COMBAT HELICOPTERS

COMBAT HELICOPTERS

Octavio Díez

Author
Octavio Díez

Collection Design
S. García

Editorial Co-ordination
E. Marín

Editorial project
2006 © UDYAT S.L.

ISBN: 84-931055-2-X
Legal deposit: B-9-343-2006

Printed in Spain

COMBAT HELICOPTERS

INDEX

ATTACK AND TRANSPORT
HELICOPTERS

The helicopter has become one of the main weapons of the 21st century, especially as it can carry out many types of missions, from the destruction of armored formations to tactical transport of special forces using stealth technology that makes detection almost impossible.

Technical improvements

The latest models that are coming on to the market, and those that are still in the development phase, use the most advanced design and manufacturing technologies. They are the result of a careful process of conception and incorporate technical solutions that reduce maintenance and the costs of manufacturing, as well as making them easier to use, even in the worst conditions.

Intelligent solutions

During the first decade of the 21st century, various models of helicopters will enter service, including:
  - The Comanche reconnaissance and attack helicopter.
  - The NH-90 medium-range transport helicopter.
  - The Agusta Bell 139 multi-role helicopter, which can be adapted for particular tasks.
These models are the result of a sustained industrial effort during more than five decades,

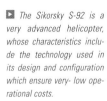 The Sikorsky S-92 is a very advanced helicopter, whose characteristics include the technology used in its design and configuration which ensure very- low operational costs.

◀ The Comanche reconnaissance and combat helicopter represents the latest advance in the development of machines with stealth technology which allows avoidance of enemy detection systems and greater mission safety.

which has resulted in an offer that ranges from light helicopters to those capable of lifting more than twenty tons.

The customer must be kept satisfied, because increasingly production runs are shorter and the costs of production are greater. In this context, it is essential to get the most out of each design, offering from the basic design as many solutions as the client needs both in conventional versions and specialized models.

Industrial power

Different American firms lead the productive helicopter sector, although the Europeans are not lagging behind and are offering increasingly more interesting and successful solutions. Both Americans and Europeans, together with some companies from the former Soviet Union – who offer very robust, but technically inferior models –, are immersed in a process of total renovation of their ranges. These include models evolved from helicopters than have been in service for two or three

decades and, in contrast, revolutionary solutions to attract potential purchasers. All these products have one common denominator: they combine the most advanced technologies available with high costs, that can range from the 4,000,000 € that a simple light helicopter might cost to the 40,000,000 € paid for a model with anti-submarine capacities, or even more if the weaponry and equipment is especially sophisticated.

A large market

Various recent conflicts, such as those in 2002 in Afghanistan and in 2003 in Iraq, have shown that the helicopter, in spite of its vulnerability, continues to be essential in military planning.

Potential sales

The developed countries are aware of the helicopter's potential, and usually included fleets of different sizes in their armies, navies and air forces. However, there are recent ideas, such as that adopted by the British, that propose a wider concept,

with helicopters satisfying different roles in function of the tasks that are required. The medium-sized countries usually have between 100 and 200 helicopters, while the United States possesses more than two thousand. This, together with the signing of various contracts in recent years, suggests a market potential of some hundreds of helicopters a year if all the different options are included. Detailed analysis shows that the largest growth area will be in transport helicopters, especially those modified for special tasks.

Attack helicopters continue to be important in countries with large budgets. Anti-submarine helicopters are evolving towards wider naval duties, while light helicopters now incorporate solutions that allow them to be used for training new pilots, linking missions or even for transporting VIPs. In summary, in the coming decades, the helicopter as we know it today will continue to be used but with improved performance and characteristics, including innovatory rotors, stealth designs and fuel-saving engines.

THE APACHE
COMBAT HELICOPTER

Designed as a helicopter with the capacity to neutralize multiple surface targets, the Apache had their baptism of fire during the Gulf War, participated in the Afghanistan War and were one of the key elements in the war against Iraq in 2003.

Perceived threat

The importance of the large number of tanks and armored cars possessed by the former Warsaw Pact countries led American strategists to conceive an armed helicopter that could halt a hypothetical advance of Soviet forces.

Design

After a long period of development and modification of components, the first helicopter was finished in the Mesa factory in Arizona, on the 30th September, 1983, and was delivered to the US Army on the 26th January, 1984. The first eleven helicopters were paid for under the 1982 budget and were first used operationally by the 6th Cavalry Regiment in July, 1986.

◄ *The Apache's most powerful weapons are the sixteen Hellfire missiles which can hit moving surface targets.*

▼ *The computerized weapon-launching system determines which threats are the most dangerous and should be dealt with first.*

Improvements

Around 800 Apache have been made for the US Army, and these are being updated to the AH-64D Longbow standard under the program begun in August, 1990. The characteristics of the new version have been validated after the evaluation of various prototypes. A large part of the US Army fleet will be updated, with the first helicopters being delivered by Boeing in March, 1997.

Capacity

Countries using the Apache include Israel, Saudi Arabia, Egypt, Greece, the United Arab Emirates, the Netherlands and the United Kingdom. Kuwait and Spain have also ordered helicopters, bringing the total ordered to date to over one thousand.

Design

With a robust configuration that improves performance and increases capacity, the new helicopters have been designed using advanced techniques that:

- Increase the safety of the pilot and copilot / gunner.

- Improve the range of weaponry.
- Improve protection against light and anti-air weapons.
- Improve the capacity to survive accidents or forced landings at speeds of up to 12.8 m/s, thanks to the Menasco landing gear, which has a large impact-absorption capacity.

Both crewmembers have various systems at their disposition:
- The tandem cockpit is strongly armored and capable of resisting perforating projectiles of 12.70x99 mm, including the 23 mm of Soviet origin.
- Flight helmets with integrated data presentation and guidance systems.
- Multipurpose data presentation screens.
- A navigation system that includes altitude radar, laser-threat radar, aerial data radar, INS, Doppler-pulse radar and GPS (Global Positioning by Satellite) systems.
- Two GE T700-GE-701C engines each with 1,890 shp of thrust, making the helicopter highly agile.

In combat
The most modern variant of this American helicopter can operate both at day and night and in the worst weather conditions, thanks to:
- Laser, infrared and other high-technology systems that allow detection, classification and prioritization of targets to be tracked and attacked.

◀ *Each of the two stub wings can house eight Hellfire missiles as well as reserve fuel tanks and other weapons.*

▶ *The radar antenna located above the rotor is the most striking visual characteristic of the D version Longbow. The millimeter-wave radar emitter is located in the interior of the housing.*

- A millimeter-wave radar, mounted on the mast over the main rotor, capable of presenting up to 256 targets on the tactical situation screen.
- A TADS/PNVS target acquisition and designation system mounted in the nose.
- An SN/ALQ-211 SIRFC Suite of Integrated RF Countermeasures System which complements the radar and laser emissions warning systems.
- AN/ALQ-144a infrared interference.

- M-130 chaff-flare dispensers.

The normal weaponry includes:
- A McDonnell Douglas M230 Chain Gun capable of firing 30 mm shells with a firing-rate of 625 per minute.
- 16 RF Hellfire anti-tank missiles.
- Rocket launchers of 2.75 inches.
- Light air-to-air missiles with infrared self-guidance.

▲ The various sensors incorporated in the AH-64 make it the best attack helicopter in the world, although the combat performance has not always been satisfactory.

▶ The automatic fire-control system makes life easier for the pilots, enabling them to fight by day or night and even in the worst weather conditions.

Technical Characteristics AH-64D

Cost (in millions of dollars):	20 millions
Size:	
Length	15,47 m
Height	4,95 m
Width	5,23 m
Main rotor turning surface	168,11 m²
Tail rotor turning surface	6,13 m²
Weight:	
Empty	5.352 kg
Maximum	10.107 kg
Maximum external load	2.712 kg
Internal fuel	1.421 l
External fuel	3.484 l
Engines:	2 GE T700-GE-701C engines with a total output of 3,780 shp
Performance:	
Service ceiling	6.400 m
Hover ceiling	4.115 m
Maximum speed	261 km/h
Range	407 km
Ferry range	1.899 km
Design load factor	+3,5/-0,5 g's

THE BO-105

The small BO-105 helicopter have shown their flexibility and capacity to adapt to various tasks and carry out a wide variety of civil, police and military missions. It is used for surveillance by law enforcement agencies in cities such as New York and Barcelona. In contrast, it has an anti-tank role in the German and Swedish armies and is also used to patrol Mexican and Chilean territorial waters.

Evolution

The German firm Messerschmitt-Bölkow-Blohm (MBB) began, after the Second World War, to design various helicopters, with the BO-105 being the first to fly, on the 16th February, 1967. In 1974, it was chosen by the German army, who maintained it in service until its substitute, the Tiger, was ready.

Exports

The Spanish army received some helicopters from Germany and decided to manufacture another 80 rotorcraft under license by Construcciones Aeronáuticas S.A. (CASA) in their Getafe factory, which also manufactured a large part of the fifty planes exported to Iraq. In addition, at the end of 1984, Sweden chose the BO-105 as the platform for the Saab-Emerson/TOW system, which has been exported to Columbia, Brunei, Indonesia, the Netherlands, Canada, Mexico, the Philippines, Peru, Nigeria, Chile and South Korea. Around 1,300 helicopters have been built or licensed to serve in around forty countries.

▼ *Germany has used the BO-105 for anti-tank duties for more than two decades. The HOT missiles can neutralize any tank within a range of 4 km.*

Possibilities

- The characteristics and agility of the BO-105 make it ideal for certain special duties that do not require a large loading capacity.
- The low noise level is useful for law enforcement agencies, both for surveillance in cities or for infiltrating special forces, who travel hanging in pairs from each side of the landing skids.
- The BO-105 can be used in many distinct military duties.
- The special variants include the naval versions with nose-mounted radar and a crane to lift small loads, and even an auxiliary fuel tank.

Design

Conceived as a compact helicopter which would be easy to maintain, the BO-105 continues to serve in a wide variety of situations and to be used by many different types of pilots, who emphasize its ease of use, evehough its power is somewhat lacking for certain tasks.

Configuration

- The fuselage comprises the main element, which is occupied in the front part by the cockpit and in the rear by the engine and the spar supporting the tail rotor.
- The two pilots sit in the front part of the cockpit and work with a central T-shaped

console, which offers all the data associated with the engines and the flight equipment.
- Behind the pilots is a three-seat bench that can be removed to accommodate small cargoes and a rear hold that is accessed by two rear doors.
- The lower part of the fuselage houses the two skids that form the landing gear.

Engine

- The CB variant has two Allison 250-C20B engines with a maximum continuous combined power of 800 shp, and an absolute maximum of 840 shp.
- The characteristics of the rotor include a titanium rotor head and four reinforced plastic blades linked to the head with no type of shock-absorption. The rotor has a 10,000-hour lifetime and can fly for 200 hours after being perforated by light weaponry.
- The fuel tanks are housed under the main cockpit and are filled by an inlet to the rear on the left side of the helicopter. The total capacity is 570 liters.

Tank hunter

The BO-105 has been adapted to act as the principal anti-tank air weapon of the armies of Germany and Spain. For this reason, an SFIM APX M397 stabilized gyro visor has been fixed to the upper part of the cockpit. The helicopters carry six heavy, anti-tank, long-range second-generation HOT missiles, housed in triple lateral banks, with a range of 4 km. The Swedish helicopters are armed with American TOW missiles.

▼ *Although small, the BO-105 can carry six anti-tank missiles, with a corresponding loss in maneuverability.*

Technical Characteristics BO-105CB

Cost (in millions of dollars):	6 millions
Size:	
Length	11,86 m
Height	3,02 m
Diameter main rotor	9,84 m
Diameter tail rotor	1,90 m
Tail rotor turning surface	76,05 m²
Weight:	
Empty	1.277 kg
Maximum	2.500 kg
Maximum load	500 kg
Internal fuel	570 l
Engines:	2 Allison 250-C20B engines with a total output of 840 shp
Performance:	
Service ceiling	3.050 m
Maximum speed	242 km/h
Endurance	596 km

AH-1 SUPER COBRA
THIRTY YEARS OF EVOLUTION

Very agile and maneuverable, due to its two-blade main rotor, the Super Cobra has been widely used in conflicts such as Vietnam, the Lebanon, Granada, Panama, and the Gulf Wars, where their robustness and compact capabilities have been proven.

A necessary rotorcraft

The Super Cobra was born as the commercial D-225 Iroquois Warrior in June, 1962, although the requirements of the US Army AAFSS (Advanced Aerial Fire Support System) program saw it evolve to the concept known as Model 209, whose prototype first flew on the 7th September, 1965.

Development

The model was accepted by the US Army on the 7th April, 1966, with the first AH-1G Cobra being sent to Vietnam in August, 1967.

The course of the war led the US Marine Corps to adopt the model in an improved two-engine version, designated the AH-1J Sea Cobra, in 1969.

The construction of around two thousand Cobra helicopters, which have been bought by Israel, Turkey, Greece, Iran, Jordan, Pakistan, Spain, Bahrain, South Korea, Thailand and Japan, among others, is due to:

- The introduction of new capabilities such as TOW wire-guided missiles.
- The incorporation of more powerful engines.
- Improved avionics.

▲ The fuselage of the Super Cobra has a smaller radar signature making detection difficult, as well as being lighter than earlier models.

◀ The agility and design of the Cobra allows it to fly in very close-formation, making detection difficult and improving survivability.

The Cobra Family

The Cobra range signifies a long evolution adapted to changing military needs.

The first model to enter service was the AH-1G, followed by advanced variants that received designations such as CONFICS, ALLD, ATAFCS or SMASH, depending on the radar systems installed.

The next advance was the AH-1Q with TOW and AH-1S missile-launching capacity and more-powerful engines that increased the craft's agility and maneuverability.

The US Marine Corps have bought a twin-engine version designated as the Sea Cobra, of which various variants have been made, including the modern Super Cobra which has been completely redesigned and now has a four-bladed rotor. The transformation will continue until 2013.

Super Cobra

Designed for the US Marine Corps, the AH-1Z is the most-powerful model in the range, with the twin engines conferring notable survivability and increased agility.

Characteristics

- The Super Cobra has a very narrow fuselage with makes frontal detection difficult and reduces the radar and infrared signature.
- It has a twin cockpit, with the pilot seated to the rear in an elevated position for greater visibility, and the copilot/systems operator seated in the front cockpit. Both cockpits incorporate screens compatible with the use of night vision goggles, have side- and belly-protection against light weapons, and are air-conditioned.
- The main rotor is located in the centre and moves the large four-blade propeller. It is powered by two General Electric T700-GE-401C engines with a total power of 3,380 shp.
- The equipment includes: Kaiser frontal data-presentation for the pilot; AN/APN-194 altimeter radar; AN/APR-47 missile warning unit; AN/ALE-47 chaff-flare dispensers; Teledyne AN/APN-21 navigation system based on Doppler pulse radar or data-encryption linked communications.

▼ *The impressive weaponry of the AH-1Z includes a three-barrel 20 mm gun and six wing stations for all types of missiles and other systems.*

Capacity

The inclusion of a modified M65 visor with a NTSF-65 Night Targeting System gives the Super Cobra 24-hour operating capacity and advanced weapons capabilities, which include:

- The General Electric GTK4A/A Universal turret in the nose, which includes a triple M197 mount with three 20 mm guns.

- The helicopter has six wing stations which can contain: 70 mm rocket-launchers; CBU-55B fuel/air explosive device pods; M118 grenade-launchers; GPU-2A or SUU-11A/A pods for multi-barrel Minigun 7.62x51 mm machine guns; and TOW or AGM-114 Hellfire anti-tank missiles.

This formidable arsenal makes the Cobra ideal for escort or armed reconnaissance missions or for attacking mechanized or armored formations.

▲ *More than a dozen countries have incorporated the Cobra over recent decades and it has been used in combat by Israel and America with great success.*

Technical Characteristics AH-1Z Super Cobra	
Cost (in millions of dollars):	18 millions
Size:	
Length	13,87 m
Height	4,39 m
Rotor diameter	14,63 m
Rotor turning surface	168,11 m²
Weight:	
Empty	5.580 kg
Maximum	8.391 kg
Maximum load weapons and fuel	2.812 kg
Internal fuel	1.565 l
Engines:	2 General Electric T700-GE-401C engines each producing 1,690 shp
Performance:	
Service ceiling	4.495 m
Maximum speed	298 km/h
Cruisisng speed	265 km
Range	705 km

THE GAZELLE
EUROPEAN HELICOPTER

The design of the Gazelle complied with strict requirements with respect to combat capacity, weapons systems, reliability, ease of maintenance and reduced operational costs.

Structure

- The teardrop-shaped fuselage has a round glassed-in cockpit and landing skids. The tapering tail boom mid-mounted on the fuselage has a swept-back tail fin, which is tapered with a square tip and rectangular flats with small fins. The fan rotor housing in built into the lower tail.
- The three-blade main rotor is mounted on the fuselage to the rear of the rotor shaft and has a prominent, upturned exhaust.

◄ *The Gazelle is the result of a joint French-British project, and is a light helicopter with great potential, especially for armed reconnaissance missions.*

▲ *The Gazelle has been widely used in combat, including Operation Iraqi Freedom in 2003.*

- External stores can be mounted on side-racks on the fuselage. Each rack has one hardpoint.
- The helicopter is powered by a Turbomeca Astazou IIIA producing 590 shp in the first variant and 890 shp in the upgraded version carried by the SA 342 which distributes exhaust gases upwards due to the IR signature suppressor on the engine exhaust.

Configuration

- Pilot and copilot are seated in the cockpit, which has a wide field of vision.
- The three bench seats in the cabin area can be folded down to leave a completely open cargo area. The cargo floor has tiedown rings.
- The weaponry installed depends on the mission, but can include mounts on both sides of the fuselage which can house containers for f 68 mm or 2.75" rocket launchers or HOT or TOW anti-tank missiles. The French helicopters have light 20 mm guns and anti-helicopter Matra Mistral missiles on double mounts, with recent models being equipped with the Viviane visor located over the cockpit.

◄ The air-to-air missiles, located in double mounts on the sides of the fuselage provides protection against other aircraft.

▼ The Gazelle's combat capacity is notable, although it lacks the armor of attack helicopters. It can be used for support missions and should remain in service for some time to come.

▲ *The Gazelle's multi-mission capacity and potential has led to them being deployed in amphibian vessels, both in combat and in peace-keeping operations.*

Technical Characteristics SA-342 Gazelle

Cost (in millions of dollars):	6 millions
Size:	
Length	11,97 m
Height	3,18 m
Width main rotor	10,50 m
Main rotor turning surface	86,50 m²
Weight:	
Empty	917 kg
Maximum	1.900 kg
Maximum external load	700 kg
Fuel	445 l
Engines:	1 Turbomeca Astazou XIV engine producing 890 shp
Performance:	
Service Ceiling	4.300 m
Maximum speed	310 km/h
Climb speed	8,5 m/s
Maximum range	755 km

THE TIGER
ATTACK HELICOPTER

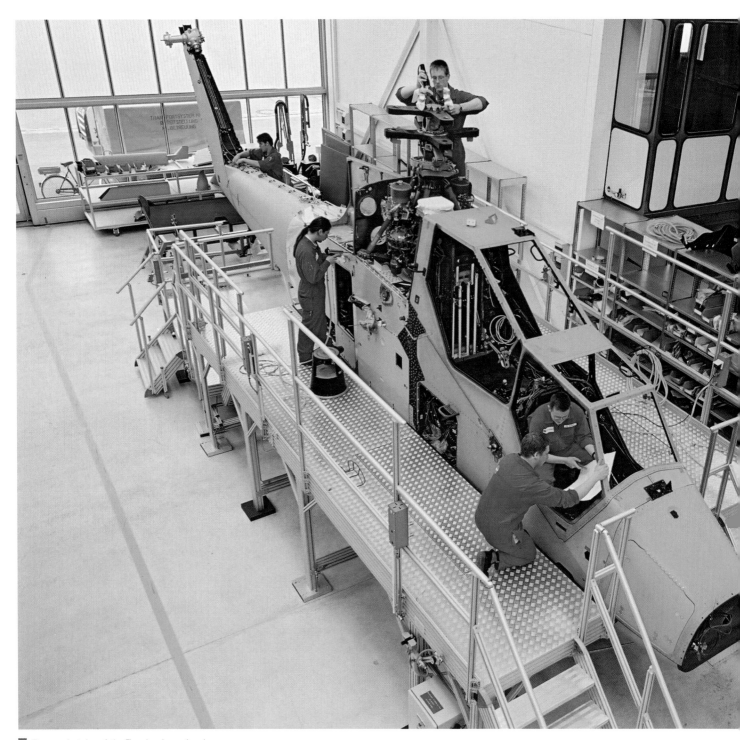

▲ The manufacturing of the Tiger has been proportionally by the participating nations according to the number ordered, with Australia receiving some recompense for its decision to participate.

The agility of the Tiger is one of its greatest qualities, increasing its survivability.

The needs of the French and German armies and defense industries for a new helicopter led to the development of the Tiger attack helicopter by the international Eurocopter company as an advanced answer to the current demand for specialized rotorcraft.

Conception

The French and German governments began to discuss a new attack helicopter in 1984, but no firm decision was taken until the 13th November, 1987. The development contract was signed on the 30th November, 1989 with the international Eurocopter company composed basically of the French Aerospatiale and the German Messerschmit Bölkow Blohm (MBB).

Evaluation and purchases

The first prototype had its first flight on the 27th April, 1991, and four others were completed by the 21st February, 1997.
As well as static tests (vibration testing, fuselage testing and verification of equipment, etc,),

29

flight tests including the launching of HOT-2 missiles were carried out. In addition, the Tiger was validated for Arctic conditions, with the PT4 undergoing tests in Sweden equipped with skids under the wheels for landing and take-off from ground at -30° c.

The good results obtained led to the signing of a production contract on the 30th June, 1995, with the first deliveries being made in 2003. During this period, the Mistral air-to-air missiles and the front gun have been validated and tests carried out to ensure the craft's suitability to fly in Australia, which has ordered 20 Aussie Tiger.

In addition, a hundred Tiger have been ordered by the French and almost two hundred, initially, by Germany. Spain may buy between 12 and 18 after expressing their desire to produce the helicopter under license on equal terms with the other partners in the program.

Possibilities

The Tiger has shown, in the many tests it has undergone, that its capabilities correspond to what was expected, namely a design that incorporates the latest technological advances allowing the helicopter to fulfill many different missions.

Advanced

The Tiger uses the most advanced technology:
- The airframe is about 80% constructed of composite materials, with the frame and beams made of Kevlar and carbon laminates and the panel of Nomex honeycomb material with skins of carbon and Kevlar, making the helicopter crashworthy at 10.5 m/s.
- The two MTU/Rolls-Royce/Turbomeca MTR390 produce 1,285 shp each, or up to 1,558 shp in emergencies, with an IR suppressor fitted to the engine exhaust.
The original design was for an attack helicopter capable of combating present and future threats in all environments, but later developments mean it is also suitable for armed reconnaissance and escort duties.

▲ *The Tiger attack helicopter can fulfill many missions, from air-to-surface to air-to-air, depending on the weapons installed.*

Cockpit

- Designed to reduce the work-load of the crew, the Tiger is fitted with a dual cockpit, with the pilot seated behind and above the gunner.
- The helicopter incorporates the latest advances in avionics including color multifunction display screen, CDU (control display units), AFCS (automatic flight control systems), ICS (intercommunication systems), RFI (radio-frequency indicators), threat-warning screens and weapons – control screens.
- Flight crew will be fitted with advanced flight helmets with a high-resolution TV system that displays flight and targeting data on the visor in a "see-through" fashion.
- The self-defense suite comprises a Thomson-CSF TSC 2000 system with IFF (identification friend or foe), laser-threat warning, radar-threat warning and chaff-flare dispensers, etc.
- The offensive power of the Tiger includes a 30mm gun turret, while the stub wings can carry missiles, rockets and other systems. Consideration is being given to include a latest-generation fiber-optic guided missile system after the cancellation of the Trigat-LR Fire and Forget missile system originally planned.

▼ *Currently, three countries have ordered the Tiger, although more sales are envisaged. Spain is on the point of signing an order.*

Technical Characteristics Tigre	
Coste (in millions of dollars):	20-30 depending on the variant
Size:	
Length	14,00 m
Height	4,32 m
Diameter main rotor	13,00 m
Main rotor turning surface	132,70 m²
Diameter tail rotor	2,70 m
Size:	
Empty	3.300 kg
Maximum	6.000 kg
Maximum load	1.660 kg
Internal fuel	1.360 l
Engines:	2 MTU/Rolls-Royce/Turbomeca MTR390 engines each producing 1,285 shp
Performance:	
Service ceiling	2.000 m
Cruising speed	280 km/h
Maximum range	800 km

NH-90
21ST CENTURY HELICOPTER

◀ *The cockpit of the NH-90 is very advanced and is conceived so that only one pilot is necessary. The multifunction displays simplify operations and lessen the work-load.*

The needs of various countries to renew the helicopter fleets then in service led to a joint-venture between Germany, France, Italy and the Netherlands to build a new multi-role naval and tactical transport helicopter of the nine-ton class.

The helicopter received the NATO designation of NH-90, which refers to the decade when it was expected to enter service, although delays now mean that the first models will be delivered in 2004.

Joint-venture

The production contract, from design to production and logistic support, was awarded to NH Industries, which has a participation of 28.2% of the Italian Agusta company, 41% of the French Eurocopter, 23.7% of the German Eurocopter Deutschland and 6.5% of the Dutch Fokker, ratios proportional to the number of helicopters each nation proposes to buy.

▼ *The NH-90 –NHF naval variant is designed to operate from frigates with a small landing pad, with its main missions being anti-submarine warfare and control of surface targets.*

Two variants

The first of four prototypes had its maiden flight on the 18th December, 1995 and since then the program of validation of equipment and capacities has continued. The NH-90 is being developed in two variants.

1ª TTH (Tactical Transport Helicopter):
  - Designed for tactical transport of personnel and material.
  - The TTH can carry between 14 and 20 soldiers who enter from the rear. It can carry two and a half tons of equipment and can participate in MEDEVAC (medical evacuation), paratroop and search and rescue operations, among others.

2ª NFH (Naval Frigate Helicopter):
  - The NFH was developed to meet the need for a ship-borne helicopter for anti-submarine and surface warfare, but can also be employed for search and rescue, vertical refueling and troop transport.

Basic Characteristics

  - The two variants are, with some differences, very similar in their general characteristics, sharing the same fuselage, engines and basic configuration.
  - The cockpit is equipped with and a multifunction display for flight, missions systems and maintenance data for the pilot, tactical coordinator and, in the naval version, the radar officer.
  - The cargo area has easy access from the rear, with equipment depending on the variant.

Germany has ordered around eighty NH-90, of which fifty will be used by the army and thirty by the air force.

The NFH is a ship-borne helicopter with various missions with up to four hours of autonomy.

- The NH-90 has two Rolls Royce Turbomeca RTM 322-01/9 or General Electric T700/T6E1 engines, chosen by each country depending on their logistic and maintenance needs.

Successful testing

All the evaluation tests have followed a very strict validation program which has exhaustively tested elements such as the titanium rotor hub with four composite blades or the integrated avionics system based on a dual digital data-bus with a color LCD.

Dual service

The sensors of both variants have also been rigorously tested, although the NFH has more sophisticated equipment to satisfy the demands of naval missions that range from surface ship attack to landings on frigates in bad-weather conditions. Other details tested include:
  - The Fly-by-Wire electronic flight control system.
  - Easy and rapid maintenance with an automatic diagnostic system that reduces the time to 2.5 maintenance man hours per flying hour.
  - Multiple redundancy of all vital systems.

Deliveries

Germany has ordered 80 helicopters which will be delivered from 2004 onwards, a date which will also see the first deliveries of the 116 ordered by Italy. In 2005, France will receive 27 helicopters. The Netherlands hopes to receive 20 NH-90 from 2007 onwards.

In addition, 10 NH-90 were ordered in June, 2001 by Portugal, Sweden has ordered 25, Finland 20, and Norway 24. These countries have also signed options for an additional number of helicopters in the future. The list of clients also includes Greece and Spain who have ordered a substantial number.

▲ *The Mil Mi-8 was conceived as a transport helicopter, but has evolved to multiple capacities including the transport of various weapons systems to combat surface threats.*

During the Lasting Freedom campaign in Afghanistan, an American Chinook helicopter was downed. To rescue it, it was decided to contract the largest helicopter available, the Russian Mil Mi-26, which can lift cargoes of more than 12 tons.

Performance

The helicopters now offered by the Russian firm Mil MHP and produced by Rostvertol PLC, which took over the from the former Soviet manufacturers, who had sold thousands of Mil helicopters, are very interesting and have some details which make them superior in some respects to their Western equivalents.

Transport capacity

The name Mil refers to Mikhail Leontyevich Mil, a Soviet engineer who became famous for due to the craft he designed during the 1960s and 1970s:
  - The Mil Mi-6, heavy transport helicopter, known as the Hook in reference to their enormous rotor and to the capacity to carry an internal cargo of 12 tons.
  - The Mil Mi-8, which has a central rotor with five enormous blades. The fuselage has two sliding doors to ease the entry and exit of troops and have a fixed landing gear which allows all-terrain landing and resistance to light impacts.
  - The Mi-8PP, equipped with sophisticated electronic interference systems.
  - The Mi-8 AMTS, the last variant of the Hip, which is armor-plated.

▲ Afghan fighters downed a number of Mil Mi-24 Hind using American missiles. The helicopter continues to serve in a significant number of countries.

▲ The Mil Mi-24 has been adapted to different environments, as it is used by many nations, especially former-Soviet Block countries. The current upgraded version is designated the Mi-35.

▲ The stub-wing mounts of the Hind can house anti-tank missiles, guns, rocket-containers and other weapons systems, leaving room in the interior hold for small troop contingents.

Greater capacity

- The Mi-17, introduced at the beginning of the 1980s as a heavily upgraded version of the Mi-8, with a troop-carrying capacity of 30 and a speed of around 250 km/h.

- The Mil Mi-26 Halo, with substantially more capacity, whose first prototype had its maiden flight in 1977. Several variants of the Mi-26, which has the largest capacity of any helicopter in service today, have been produced.

- The Mi-26T, the latest variant of the Mi-26 has a modernized cockpit and can fulfill various missions of transport of troops and material, including making use of the cargo sling.

Armored targets

One of the greatest successes of Mil has been the range of combat helicopters, especially those conceived for armored targets.

Proven effectiveness

The Russian-Afghan War demonstrated the qualities of the Mi-24 Hind, which aroused the interest of the Americans so much that they mounted a complex rescue mission to recover a Libyan craft which had been abandoned in Chad. The Mi-24 Hind has some special features not possessed by other models:

- A dual cockpit which gives the pilots a very-wide field of vision.

- The fuselage is stretched to improve the interior cargo load of troops or additional fuel.

- The craft has two stub wings with mounts for rocket-launchers, anti-tank missiles and even anti-air systems.

The latest version of the Hind is the Mi-35 which has a performance which may keep it flying for another 15 or 20 years, although such considerations must take into account

▶ *The appearance of the Apache led to a rapid Soviet response, the Mil Mi-28. The picture shows the engines and the radar antenna mounted over the rotor.*

the very long useful flying lives of these helicopters conceived in the former Soviet Union.

New model

To complement and later replace the Hind, Mil developed the Mi-28 Havoc, the latest of a series of helicopters of which more than 30,000 have been sold in the last four decades. Design work began 1980 and four prototypes were constructed, one of which was presented in the West at the Le Bourget Air Show in 1989, to great surprise. In 1996, the Mi-28N day and night capable variant prototype was produced, which incorporates a microwave radar antenna mounted above the rotor head.

The mission of the Mi-28 is to destroy armored and other combat material, low and slow-flying airborne vehicles and other battlefield targets. To date, there have been no export or-ders, and some helicopters are maintained in service in the Russian armed forces. These may have been combat-evaluated to verify their capacity to resist light-weapons impacts and validate their versatility in especially complex situations.

◢ *The Mil Mi-8 are excellent transport helicopters, with more than two decades of service behind them and possibly another two to come.*

Technical Characteristics Mi-28 Havoc	
Cost (in millions of dollars):	Unknown
Size:	
Length	17,01 m
Height	4,70 m
Width	4,88 m
Diameter main rotor	17,20 m
Main rotor turning surface	232,35 m²
Size:	
Empty	8.095 kg
Maximum	11.660 kg
Internal fuel	1.665 l
Engines:	2 Klimov TV3-117VM engines producing a total of 4,140 shp
Performance:	
Service ceiling	5.800 m
Maximum speed	300 km/h
Tactical action radius	200 km
Ferry range	1.100 km
Design load factor	+3/-0, 5 g's

THE UH-1
FOUR DECADES OF ACTIVITY

The different versions of the UH-1, which were widely used to transport troops and materiel during the Vietnam War, have demonstrated their capacity to comply with all the missions demanded of a light, military utility helicopter. More than 16,000 have been manufactured to date.

Conception

In 1955, the US Army, after the experience of the Korean War commissioned the building of a new utility helicopter to evacuate troops from the front line. The Bell company was chosen to build what was designated the Model 204.

Initial evolution

After the first flight of the XH-40 on the 22nd October, 1956, a rapid test period led to the construction of some six evaluation models.

These were followed by nine pre-series UH-1
that could transport six troops.

Popularly known as the Huey, (for HU, helicopter utility) deliveries of the first UH-1A
to the US Army began on the 30th June 1959
and were completed in March, 1961. The
variants included:

- The Slick, troop transport.
- The Hog, artillery variant.
- The Iroquois, multi-role model H.

The UH-1B variant with a more powerful
engine was delivered from 1961 onwards

and was followed by :

- The 767 helicopters of the model C .
- The 2, 201 craft of the model D.
- The E variant, modified tooperate from
amphibious assault ships.
- The F model used by the US Air Force.
- The 5,345 H model helicopters made for the
US Army with a stretched fuselage and more
powerful engine.

The most recent variant is the UH-1Y produced by Bell Helicopter Textron and adapted
for the US Marine Corps, which has two

engines, nose-mounted FLIR (forward-looking infrared) and other details that will allow it to remain operative until 2030.

The H model has had the greatest success and has the most helicopters in service. Their instrument screens have been modified for use with night vision goggles and there have been changes in the equipment. From the original model several variants, identified by the designation letter, have been configured:
- The T model, used as advanced instrument trainers.
- The E electronic warfare model.
- The H search and rescue model.
- The R research model.

There have also been Twin Pac engine models such as the UH-1N and AB-212, and a four-blade variant, the Bell 412.

The Huey has fulfilled diverse missions in more than fifty countries including the United States, Brunei, Finland, Norway, Spain and Uruguay. In recent years, the United States has given many helicopters to friendly South-American countries.

Design concept
The Huey design is based on a fuselage with a wide transversal section constructed of light alloys and, with the exception of the 412, using a semi-rigid rotor with two articulated blades.

Innovative
The Huey was the first series helicopter to use an engine mounted over the fuselage very close to the main rotor assembly, giving it a larger cargo hold.

The configuration includes:
- A frontal cockpit for the pilot and copilot.
- A central cargo hold for troop or materiel transport.
- A tail spar inclined upwards with a tail rotor.
- Landing gear facilitating all-terrain landings.

The normal capacity of the H model is twelve completely equipped soldiers, litters, or two tons of cargo, either in the hold or in the cargo sling. The Huey has participated in the Arab-Israeli wars, the invasion of Grenada and in the peace-keeping operations in Kurdistan.

Combat adapted
The weaponry which can be included varies from the Marte MK-2 anti-ship missiles carried by the Italian Griffon to the array of machine guns used against the Colombian guerillas.

In the utility variants, mounts can be installed:
- In the internal hold, including mounts for medium and heavy machine guns, automatic grenade-launchers, or Minigun machine guns.
- On exterior mounts which can contain all type of unguided rocket-launchers and even anti-tank missiles.

▲ The Huey, as these helicopters are known, are reliable, robust and very efficient, although some of the older models are beginning to show their age.

Technical Characteristics UH-1H	
Cost (in millions of dollars):	6 millions
Size:	
Length	13,59 m
Height	4,41 m
Rotor diameter	14,63 m
Main rotor turning surface	168,10 m²
Weight:	
Empty	2.363 kg
Maximum	4.309 kg
Maximum external load	2.000 kg
Internal load	945 l
Engines:	One Lycoming T53-L-13 engine producing 1,400 shp
Performance:	
Service ceiling	3.840 m
Maximum speed	204 km/h
Low-level flying range	512 km
Range with auxiliary tanks, flying at 1,120 m	800 km

THE UH-60
THE MOST VERSATILE MILITARY HELICOPTER

The Black Hawk helicopter is a direct result of the lessons learned in the Vietnam War. It is a multi-mission medium-weight helicopter, adapted to modern requirements, with many versions being produced for different countries.

Requirements

The origins of the Black Hawk lie in the publication of the UTTAS (Utility Tactical Transport Aircraft System) study, which argued the need for a new medium-weight transport helicopter.

Development

During 1974 and 1975, prototypes from Boeing Vertol and Sikorsky Aircraft were evaluated. On the 23rd December, 1976 the Sikorsky YUH-60A was chosen and a first order of 15 helicopters was signed.

Designated the UH-60A Black Hawk, the first units were delivered in 1979 to the 101st Air Transport Division based at Fort Campbell in Kentucky. At that time, around ten helicopters were being produced every month and, to date, more than two thousand have been constructed.

The initial UH-60 variant included:

- A carrying capacity of three crew and eleven fully-equipped troops.

▲ Among the Black Hawk variants produced is that used for medical evacuation which can carry four litters and a medical officer.

- Multi-mission capabilities including medical evacuation, reconnaissance, logistic support, and, with a Volcano dispenser, mine-laying capabilities, in common with the improved UH-60L version introduced in 1989.

Specific variants include:
  - The EH-60, equipped with electronic warfare systems.
  - The MH-60, equipped with weapons and systems for Special Forces Operations.
  - The HH/MG-60G Pave Hawk, for pilot-rescue missions.
  - The SH-70 Seahawk, adapted for anti-submarine and anti-surface attack missions.
  - The VH-60, for VIP transport.
  - The UH-60Q Dustoff, for armed MEDEVAC missions.

Users

The possibilities of the Black Hawk mean that it has been used for tasks as varied as carrying the President of the United States or for police surveillance in Turkey. This wide range of capacities has given rise to specially-designed variants and various export models which include:
  - The Desert Hawk, used by Saudi Arabia.
  - The S-70A-5, used by the Philippine air force.
  - The UH-60A Yanshuf, widely used by Israel in military actions.

Other countries that use variants of the Black Hawk include Egypt, Spain, Japan, Jordan, Argentina, and Morocco. In addition, they are used by various American government agencies and law enforcement agencies.

▲ The Black Hawk is configured for two relatively small
engines that be dismounted
easily for maintenance.

◄ The cockpit of the Black
Hawk is conventional, with a
pilot and copilot, but has undergone multiple upgradings.

Characteristics

The UH-60 and its derivatives have been widely used in combat in recent decades, with the Afghan and Iraq campaigns being the latest examples, demonstrating that their design characteristics enable them to successfully negotiate the requirements of the modern battlefield.

Resistent

- The fuselage incorporates materials such as titanium, Kevlar, graphite and plastic fibers, whose combination makes the Black Hawk tolerant to small arms fire and most medium caliber projectiles.
- The landing gear is energy absorbing, enabling the Black Hawk to conserve 85% of the structure after a vertical impact of 11.5 m/s, a side impact of 9.1 m/s and a longitudinal impact of 12.2 m/s.
- The blades of the main and tail rotors can resist the impact of 23 mm projectiles without major damage.
- The internal tanks have a capacity of 1,361 liters and are crash resistant and self-sealing.
- The Black Hawk is provided with redundant electric and hydraulic systems.
- The energy-absorbing crew seats are armored for additional protection.
- The belly of the cargo cabin is reinforced to resist light weapons impacts.

Survivability is aided by the Black Hawk's power and speed. Since 1989, they have been powered by two General Electric T700-GE-701C engines producing a total of 3.600 shp. The main rotor is made of titanium and has four 8 m blades, with the small tail rotor located at an angle to the vertical.

▶ *The Black Hawk can lift more than three tons of cargo using the cargo hook, allowing it to fulfill many logistic and support missions.*

Technical Characteristics UH-60L	
Cost (millions of dollars)	5,87 millions
Dimensions:	
Length fuselage	15,26 m
Height	5,13 m
Width with rotor turning	19,76 m
Cockpit volume	11,61 m³
Surface of propellers	8,68 m²
Weight:	
Empty	5.224 kg
Maximum	11.113 kg
Maximum interior load	1.197 kg
Maximum external load	3.629 kg
Internal fuel capacity	1.361 l
Combustible Maximum	6.507 l
Engine:	2 General Electric T700-GE-701C engines each producing 1800 shp
Performance:	
Service ceiling	5.837 m
Maximum speed	361 km/h
Cruising speed	294 km/h
Hover ceiling	2.895 m
Range	584 km
Ferry range	2.222 km

▲ *The naval variants are used for multiple missions including search and rescue, employing the side-winch.*

Capacity

Defined as "a helicopter designed by the military for the military" the Black Hawk has represented a real landmark for the American industry, achieving high levels of safety and operability in all combat operations in which it has participated. It is used not only by the US Army but also by the Air Force and the Navy. The main characteristics include:

- Folding and partially detachable blades and tail rotor to facilitate transport by ship or transport airplanes.
- A loading capacity which allows them to carry two infantry squads in the cargo cabin or a 105 mm light artillery piece slung from the cargo hook as well as the gunners and a supply of ammunition.
- The naval versions incorporate FLIR, variable-depth, low-frequency sonar and chaff-flare launchers controlled by display panels in the cargo cabin operated by specialized personnel. The latest model can carry a large payload of missiles, rockets, cannons and electronic countermeasures pods.

THE SEA KNIGHT
NAVAL TRANSPORT

The CH-46, widely used as an assault vector by the amphibian craft of the US Navy has demonstrated its capacity to carry out the transport of troops and equipment for the US Marine Corps for over 30 years.

Origins in the 1950s

In 1956, the American firm Vertol began design and engineering studies for a twin-turbine transport helicopter with both civil and military applications.

Development

The prototype, designated the Model 107, first flew on the 22nd April, 1958. Soon afterwards, three evaluation models of the naval variant known as the CH-46A were ordered by the US Army, although finally the CH-47 Chinook was judged superior. However, the helicopter was chosen by the U.S. Marine Corps to fulfill their need for a helicopter for amphibious assault operations.

In February, 1961, 14 CH-46A were ordered by the Marines, the first of which had its maiden flight on the 16th October, 1962. The US Navy selected the helicopter in 1964 a logistic transport helicopter and in 1965 the Japanese began manufacture of the craft under license by Kawasaki.

The first series included: 266 model D, 186

model F, and some model E produced from 1977 onwards using older craft. Specialized versions such as the HH-46D search and rescue variant and the RH-46 minehunters, the KV-107II/IIA built in Japan and exported to Saudi Arabia, the CH-113 Labrador used in Canada and an anti-submarine variant deployed by Sweden.

Improvements

The Sea Knight is nicknamed the Frog by crewmembers. Currently, around 300 CH-46E Sea Knight are still serving in the US Marine Corps and a lesser number in the US Navy, the helicopter having undergone various upgrades designed to keep them flying until the end of the present decade.

The modifications have included:

- The replacement of the rotor blades.
- Uprated engines.
- Structural reinforcements.
- The fitting of emergency sea-landing equipment.
- The addition of self-defense measures such as chaff-flare launchers and electronic

countermeasures systems.

- Low infra-red reflection paints.
- Reinforcement of some elements with armor.

These and other, lesser changes are designed to keep the Sea Knight flying until it is replaced by the V-22.

Proven design

Compact and capable, the performance of the CH-46 is limited by the outdated design.

Effective conception

- The fuselage is made of an aluminum alloy and is designed to achieve more interior space and better access for cargo and personnel. The upper part of the fuselage contains the supports for the transmission and the engines.

- A rear door and ramp gives access to the cargo hold, which contains two rows of tactical seats along the sides, with a capacity for 26 fully-equipped troops or the transport of all types of combat-support materiel, from light missile launchers to ammunition.

- The loading capacity is around four tons, thanks to

the powerful General Electric T58-GE-16 engines, an uprated version of the original engine.

- The engines turn two large three-bladed tandem rotors, one at the front and the other at the rear, which turn in opposite directions to improve stability while hovering.

- The rotor blades can be folded rapidly by a system controlled from the cockpit.

Tactics

Unlike the Vietnam War era, when helicopters flew from a high altitude to avoid being hit by light anti-air or portable weapons, current tactics include:

- TERF (Terrain Flight mission) where the helicopter flies at an altitude of between 15m and 50 m to take advantage of the uneven terrain to make location more difficult.

- NOE (Nap of the Earth Flight) where the helicopters fly at an altitude of less than 15 m using mapped corridors. To improve the possibilities of use and the capacities of the crew, regular CAX (Combined Arms eXercices) are carried out in the Twenty-nine Palms Desert, in California.

◀ *American amphibious units use the CH-46 as a basic plat-form for transport and limited air assault operations, although the helicopters have suffered a high rate of accidents.*

▲ *The fuselage of this CH-46 has a watertight belly to permit ditching for rescue purposes or to embark small craft.*

Technical Characteristics CH-46E	
Cost (millions of dollars):	16 millions
Dimensions:	
Length	13,66 m
Height	5,09 m
Rotor diameter	15,24 m
Rotor turning surface	364,60 m²
Cargo hold surface area	16,72 m²
Weight:	
Empty	5.927 kg
Maximum	10.433 kg
Maximum interior load	4.000 kg
Internal fuel capacity	3.786 l
Engine:	2 General Electric T58-GE-16 engines producing a total of 3,740 shp
Performance:	
Service ceiling	4.265 m
Maximum speed	267 km/h
Endurance	383 km

THE CHINOOK
TRANSPORT HELICOPTER

▲ One of the most visible characteristics of the Chinook is the large twin- rotor, which, combined with the noise produced by the engines make them instantly recognizable.

The Boeing CH-47 Chinook is a robust, twin-turbine, tandem-rotor, heavy-lift transport helicopter capable of lifting all types of cargoes and tested in combat from Vietnam to the Falklands War, with a high rate of availability.

Development and evolution

In 1957, the US Army began the search for a newly-designed heavy helicopter. In 1960, Boeing proposed a model designated the V-114, which became the YHC-1B and, in 1962, the CH-47 Chinook.

Capacity

The YHC-1B first flew on the 21st September, 1961 and underwent a rapid evaluation process together with other prototypes. The first series model was the CH-47a, delivered in August, 1962 to the 1st Air Cavalry Division, who took charge of a large part of the 354 helicopters of this variant produced.

On the 10th May, 1967 the CH-47B was introduced, with larger engines. In October, 1962, the CH-47C first flew, with 270 helicopters being delivered from Spring 1968. In 1973, 182 CH-47 were upgraded with new composite rotor blades, and more-rapid maintenance. In 1976, a major fleet update began, resulting in the CH-47D, which features composite rotor blades, improved electrical systems, modular hydraulics and more-powerful engines and is sched-uled to remain in service until 2025.

Combat experience has shown that the Chinook is perfectly adapted for military use and can fulfill many missions.

Specialized versions

Taking the original design as a base, and following the example of the Vietnam-era AH-47 Gunship, specialized variants have been produced, including:

- The MH-47D of the 160th Special Operations Regiment of the US Army, which are equipped with in-flight refueling capabilities, forward looking infrared, terrain-following/terrain-avoidance radar, and two multi-barrel Minigun 7.62 mm machine guns.

- The advanced Mk2 used by the Royal Air Force.

- The Mk3 assigned to the British special forces. The Spanish FAMET forces have four models for infiltration and exfiltration of special operations teams.

These modifications and the capacity of the basic design has resulted in more than a thousand Chinook being bought by countries such as Argentina, Australia, Canada, the Netherlands, South Korea, Thailand and others, with more than a thousand being made.

Notable characteristics

The size and loading capacity of the Chinook are inherent in their design and potential. Military users have many reasons to be grateful for these characteristics.

Optimized details

- The long, wide fuselage is made of metal and has a constant cross-section centre.

- The fuselage includes five small side observation windows, a large rear door and ramp to allow rapid de-embarkation of troops and equipment, and a modern cockpit with side windows that can be used as emergency exits by the pilots.

◄ *Later models of the Chinook are fitted with exterior radar-detection systems and chaff-flare launchers.*

△ *The Chinook carry electronic systems that allow precise flying including very-close formations.*

- All-weather flying is guaranteed by systems which include altitude radar, automatic stabilization, a VOR receiver, Tacan, complex HF and UHF communications systems, horizontal situation indicator, satellite links and GPS systems.
- The Chinook is powered by two AlliedSignal T55-L-712 SBB engines with 4,314 shp maximum unitary power or the 714 which increases power to 4,867 shp in an emergency. The engines turn at 225 revolutions per minute and move two large three-blade rotors.

Missions

- The large interior hold (21 m2 surface area and 41 m3 volume) means the Chinook can be configured for various personnel transport options thanks to the tactical seats integrated in the sides, which can carry up to 44 fully-equipped troops or 55 troops in emergency situations.
- The rear door allows embarkation of light vehicles, artillery or missile systems and is also used for parachute launches.
- The Chinook has triple cargo hooks with the central hook lifting 11,793 kg and the side hooks 7,711 kg each, although they are usually used in combination.
- Self-defense measures include radar-detectors, chaff-flare launchers, and mounts for heavy machine guns.

◄ The Chinook can carry two light 105 mm guns in the cargo sling, enabling the batteries to change position rapidly and make detection more difficult.

Technical Characteristics CH-47D	
Cost (millions of dollars)	30 millions
Dimensions:	
Length	30,14 m
Height	5,78 m
Rotor diameter	18,29 m
Rotor turning surface	525,30 m²
Flap surface area	2,91 m²
Weight:	
Empty	10.693 kg
Maximum	24.494 kg
Maximum load	12.284 kg
Internal fuel capacity	3.902 l
Engine:	2 Allied Signal T-55-L-714 engines producing a total of 8,336 shp
Performance:	
Service ceiling	3.095 m
Maximum speed	298 km/h
Radius of action	185 km

FROM THE STALLION
TO THE SUPER STALLION

The CH-53 is the heaviest-lifting, currently-serving Western helicopter. Its performance and mission capabilities have been proven in many fields of combat, including the rescue of civilian personal from areas in conflict to the recent CSAR operation to rescue Captain O'Grady.

Widely tested

The gestation of the Sikorsky S-65, the factory denomination of the CH-53, began in October, 1960 when the US Marine Corps began its search for a new heavy lift helicopter.

Complex program

On the 7th March, 1962 the requirements for the HH(X) (Helicopter, Heavy, eXperimental) were published, and included a configuration capable of transporting a load of 3,630 kg for a distance of 185 km. The proposals of Boeing, Kaman and Sikorsky were considered, and in September, 1962, a derivation of the Sikorsky offer was chosen.

The first YCH-53A had its maiden flight on the 14th October, 1964 and the evaluations continued without problems. The Marines received the first CH-53A in September, 1965, part of the initial batch of 141.

The production line continued with the model C for the US Air Force, the model D for the Marines and the model G, constructed under license by Germany.

The initial variants of the Sea Stallion were followed by other more-powerful models adapted to specific requirements. These included:

 - The HH-53H and MH-53J Pave Low, used by the US Air Force por pilot rescue missions.
 - The MH-53E Sea Dragon, with mine-sweeping capabilities.

 - The CH-53E Super Stallion, with three powerful engines, used by the US Marine Corps.

Improvements

Since 1991, the Israeli firm MATA, part of the Israeli Aircraft Industries Group has been upgrading the 40 Israeli helicopters to the CH-53-2000 which includes:

 - A fixed in-flight refueling nozzle.
 - Two exterior supplementary fuel tanks with a capacity of 4,000 liters.
 - New self-defense measures including chaff-flare launchers and electronic countermeasures.
 - Modified cockpit instrumentation, with multifunction display panels adapted for use wit night vision goggles.

- An increase in the maximum take-off load to 22,680 kg.

Notable capacity

Variants of the Stallion have been used in the 1991 and 2003 Gulf Wars and operations in Liberia and Albania. Specific actions include the transport of a battery of anti-aircraft missiles captured by Israeli commandos and the attempted liberation of the American hostages in Iran, which ended in failure.

Design details

- The fuselage is made of aluminum, steel and titanium.
- The cockpit is configured of a combination of glass fiber and glass.
- Some elements are reinforced with a covering of polyamide and pieces of titanium to increase resistance to impacts.
- Access is facilitated by the large dimensions of the helicopter.
- The rear door and loading ramp, together with a remotely-controlled winch at the forward end of the cargo compartment facilitate cargo handling.
- The landing gear is composed of three retractable double wheels, equipped with heavy-duty shock absorbers.
- An access door on the front of the right side that includes a winch for rescue missions or lifting small cargoes.
- The E variant is powered by three General Electric T64-GE-416 or 419 engines, equipped with air separators to reduce power loss in sandy environments.

Sophisticated equipment

Maintenance is facilitated by advanced inspections systems, with electronics that warn of breakdowns or the need to replace components.

Each variant incorporates specific systems:

- The models used by Special Operations Forces have very-low flying capabilities.
- The models with mine-sweeping capabilities are equipped with special antenna for detection of mines in difficult conditions.

All models can be fitted with air-to-air missiles for self-defense. In addition, many models are fitted with in-flight refueling systems, radar and infrared countermeasures, radar systems, heat-seeking systems, and mounts for support weapons.

◀ *Some versions of the Stallion have incorporated in-flight refueling systems, considerably increasing their range.*

▶ *The flight qualities and range of action of the Stallion allow them to fly in difficult conditions and act as troop supports in any environment. Many were used in Operation Iraqi Freedom at the beginning of 2003.*

Technical Characteristics CH-53E	
Cost (millions of dollars):	24,36 millions
Dimensions:	
Length	30,19 m
Height	8,97 m
Width	8,66 m
Main rotor turning surface	455,38 m²
Tail rotor turning surface	29,19 m²
Weight:	
Empty	15.072 kg
Maximum	33.450 kg
Maximum load	16.330 kg
Internal fuel capacity	3.849 l
External fuel capacity	4.921 l
Engine:	Three General Electric T64-GE-416 engines producing a total of 13,140 shp
Performance:	
Service ceiling	5.640 m
Maximum speed	315 km/h
Range	2.075 km

THE SUPER PUMA
AND COUGAR

The French defense industry have optimized their export-production, showing, with the Super Puma family, that they can design and build medium transport helicopters with ground, naval or air support mission capabilities.

Conception

After the sales success of the AS-330 Puma transport helicopter, of which more than 700 were built, many of which continue to fly in various countries, it was decided to develop an improved variant.

Evolution

The first design concepts were begun in 1974 and the validation prototype had its maiden flight on the 13th September, 1978. After verification tests, production began of the AS-332 Super Puma. The first examples were delivered during 1981. In July, 1983 the L variant with a stretched fuselage was introduced, and in 1986 the Turbomeca Makila 1A1 engines began to be fitted.

The military versions of the Puma, produced from 1990 onwards, were designated as the AS-532 Cougar. The EC-725 – produced by Eurocopter – are the most recent model. Ten have been ordered for the French special forces, which will be delivered between 2004 and 2006 at a cost of 271,000,000 € each.

▲ *The Super Puma is ideal for transport missions although its use for military duties is not universally praised.*

Sales

The helicopters produced in France by Aerospatiale, or those produced under license in Indonesia, Spain, Turkey or Switzerland, are identified by letters which define their characteristics and missions:

- U is used for unarmed variants.
- A is used for armed models.
- C is used for the short-bodied military model.
- L is the stretched-fuselage military model.
- S is the naval version for anti-submarine and anti-ship missions.

Nineteen-ninety-three saw the introduction of the Mk2 model, which shares a production line with the older Mk1. Almost five hundred helicopters of the series have been ordered by around 60 countries that include:

▼ *The two wide, side sliding doors make it easy to embark and disembark troops.*

- France, which has specialized models such as the Horizon battlefield detection radar transport and the Mk2 U2 assigned to CSAR (Combat Search and Rescue) missions.
- Spain, which has more than forty craft divided between the air force and army.
- Abu Dhabi, who operate five helicopters modified with sonar and AM-39 Exocet anti-ship missile and torpedo launching capacities.
- Turkey, with around twenty helicopters manufactured under license.
- Other countries such as Slovakia, the Netherlands, Panama or Mexico.

Design

The helicopters have been praised for their 98% operational effectiveness in support duties for North Sea oil rigs and criticized by military experts for their performance in day-to-day support activities. However, they have been a success and are still being produced.

Conception

- A wide-body large-capacity fuselage made of light aluminum alloy, serves as the base for a structure that includes titanium reinforcement and elements made of composite materials.
- The cockpit needs one pilot in good visibility and two for IFR flying.

▲ *The cockpit has been modernized in recent versions and now includes digital display screens.*

- The central cargo cabin holds 25 fully-equipped troops.
- The tail spar carries the tail rotor.
- The belly of the helicopter holds five fuel deposits with a capacity that ranges from 1,497 liters in the UC variant to 2,141 liters in the SC variant. If necessary, additional interior tanks holding 2000 liters can be installed in the cargo hold and two exterior tanks of 650 liters for long-range missions.
- The helicopter has two modular Turbomeca Makila 1A1 engines fitted with air intakes equipped with filters to avoid sucking in foreign bodies or ice. The Mk2 models are powered by the Makila 1A2 which produces 2,109 shp and turns the main rotor which has four articulated blades with elastomeric bearings to improve resistance to impacts and perforation. The tail rotors are made of carbon fiber, titanium and resins.

Capacity

The Puma was originally designed to carry combat-equipped troops, either with or without the use of tactical seating. The cargo capacity of 4.5 tons and other details have allowed variants which can fulfill search and rescue missions, naval defense models with anti-ship missiles, VIP transport variants, long-range models with in-flight refueling capacities and even anti-submarine versions with sonar buoys and variable-depth, low-frequency sonar.

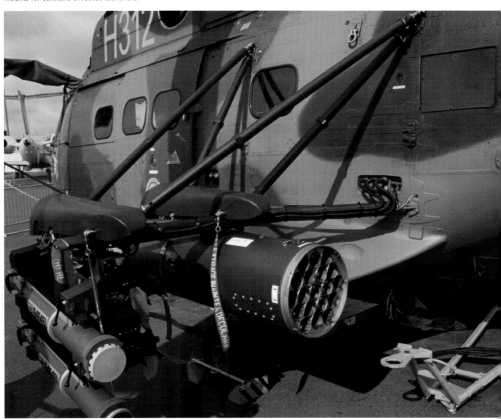

Among the variants of the Puma is this model with side mounts for cannons or rocket-launchers.

Technical Characteristics CH-AS-532SC	
Cost (millions of dollars)	14-18
Dimensions:	
Length fuselage	15,53 m
Height	4,92 m
Diameter main rotor	15,60 m
Main rotor turning surface	191,13 m²
Cockpit surface	7,80 m²
Weight:	
Empty	4.500 kg
Maximum	9.350 kg
Maximum external load	4.500 kg
Internal fuel capacity	2.141 l
Engine:	2 Turbomeca Makila 1A1 engines producing a total of 3,754 shp
Performance:	
Service ceiling	4.100 m
Hover ceiling	2.800 m
Maximum speed	278 km/h
Range	870 km

V-22
OSPREY

At first sight, many would ask themselves whether the Osprey is a helicopter or an airplane. The truth is that it is a craft that uses new technology to incorporate the advantages of VTOL with the range and speed of an airplane, combining details of both in an intelligent way.

The technical solutions provided by the Osprey design were appreciated by the American military, especially the US Marine Corps who required a new helicopter to replace the CH-46 Sea Knight. The revolutionary performance, combat capacity and other details meant that the Osprey was rapidly selected, although at present none have entered service as severe problems, including severe accidents, have occurred during the latest development phase.

Reality or fiction
The roots of the Osprey program go back to August, 1955 with the first flight of the Bell XV-3, a craft with pivoted rotors that crashed two months later. A second prototype served to advance the research program, but it was not until the middle of the 1970s when the Bell XV-15, a more advanced solution supported by the US Army and NASA was unveiled.

▲ The pre-series models are undergoing a strict development program which is trying to solve the various problems that have appeared in recent years.

◄ The large three-blade rotors of the Osprey are shown in this frontal image. The main difference with other models lies in the disposition of the engines and the dual operating capabilities.

Joint proposal

In 1981, a development program known as the JVX (Joint Services Advanced Vertical Lift Aircraft) was announced, with Bell and Boeing being awarded around 200 million dollars for development phases. Shortly afterwards, the US Navy took charge of the coordination and management of the program, which, little by little advanced until, on the 23rd May, 1988 the first prototype of the V-22 was presented in the Arlington (Texas) plant.

At that time, it was planned to construct some 800 rotorcraft which would serve all four branches of the US military and which would enter service from 1992 onwards. However, problems soon began to appear and the first flight did not take place until the spring of 1989.

Troubled development

The initial development phases were not as smooth as hoped for, in spite of the pre-development studies, and were plagued with so many incidents that at the end of the 1990s, the cancellation of the program was announced, although pressure from the United States Congress succeeded in halting the cancellation. The first prototypes were delivered and evaluation tests began. However, in 1991, one Osprey crashed and a similar accident happened in 1992.

Political pressure, military decisions and the interests of the military-industrial complex in general, marked the 1990s. The pressure to develop the Osprey has been led by the US Marine Corps, although the two crashes,

▼ *The configuration of the fuselage facilitates automatic and manual operation. The craft is very wide and the interior hold is big enough to carry loads adequate for many different missions.*

with a number of deaths have marked the evaluation phases.

Performance
The reason that the design of the Osprey has been maintained in spite of so many problems failures in the flight control system, leaks in the hydraulics systems, construction defects, etc - is that the performance is not matched by any other craft, and this justifies continuing with the project.

Basic details
- The V-22 is a VTOL rotorcraft provided with a hinged wing that has very little in common

with conventional designs.

- The two T406-AD-400 engines, with a maximum power of 6,150 shp turn the three-blade rotor.

- The nacelles rotate 90o forward (Full Vertical to Full Horizontal), varying the angle of the engines to enable vertical flight.

- The design calls for a helicopter with hinged rotors enabling it to fly as an airplane, and thus giving it greater capacity to carry out various combat missions, but using a conventional disposition for flights requiring higher sustained speed and a greater range.

- The disposition of the craft gives it a more conventional fuselage with greater internal capacity and allow easy access.

▲ The two external cargo hooks for heavy external loads allow
the V-22 to lift loads of around seven tons like a normal helicopter.

Complex solution

Another possible design feature is the concept of the wing turning on itself to become aligned
with the fuselage, thus substantially reducing the space occupied by the craft and facilitating
its storage in the hold of aircraft-carriers.

One of the main problems is that the Osprey requires a large landing space, due to the parallel configuration of the rotors. The Marines have not given much importance to this problem,
because they feel the craft's advantages outweigh the possible disadvantages.

The Osprey will include:

- In-flight refueling capabilities, although the normal range exceeds 3,000 miles.
- Radar which will allow day/night all-weather flying.
- Mounts for various weapons systems.

The Osprey will also be used by the US Air Force for long range special operations missions
and the insertion and extraction of special forces teams and equipment and the rescue of
downed pilots.

AIRBORNE
OPERATIONS

The development and evolution of models of helicopters is conditioned by the missions they must serve. Of these, that of serving as an air vector for the type of missions involving the transport of troops, materiel and weapons systems is, perhaps, the most important.

Implantation
The experiences of the Germans and Americans during the Second World War included the use of helicopters in all types of military operations.

Possible uses
During the Korean War, helicopters began to be used for a wide variety of missions. At the beginning, the Vought-Sikorsky R-5 and the Bell M47 were used for MEDEVAC duties and for observation, although the arrival of the Sikorsky S-55 meant helicopters could perform transport and rescue missions, as their cargo hold allowed the transport of squads of troops to the front line.

The American experience in Korea and that of the French in Indochina, led to the consideration of the helicopter as an Air Cavalry vehicle. This type of mission was carried out successfully by the French in Algeria using the Piasecki H-21, by the British in Cyprus using the Bristol Sycamore to fight against the EOKA guerillas, and, above all, in Vietnam, where American strategies led to the development of many types of helicopters. The UH-1 was

▼ Smaller helicopters, such as this British Lynx, can move small groups of troops rapidly and stealthily.

converted into a multifunction helicopter with missions ranging from the infiltration and exfiltration of troop squads to and from the front lines to attack using the power of their machine guns and rockets.

The helicopter became an essential part of modern warfare, carrying out rescues of downed pilots, MEDEVAC operations, logistical support missions and many other activities. The casualty rate was high, with many helicopters being shot down.

Limited assault

The first experience of the mission of helicopters as assault craft corresponded to the Spanish army who used them against the Moroccans and the Polisario Front in the first half of the 1970s. Later, the British used many helicopters in this role during the Falklands War. During the 1983 invasion of Grenada, some American assault helicopters were downed by light weapons fire.

The utility of helicopters as assault craft was also shown in the 1991 Gulf War when used by the American XVIII Army Air Transport Corps. Since then, helicopters have participated as a normal element in all offensive military actions or peace-keeping missions, especially in Afghanistan and Iraq.

Evolution of the doctrine

The doctrine of using the helicopter in airborne operations has evolved according to the appearance of new models, missions and operative requirements.

▼ *The fast rope technique is a comfortable, simple and very safe way of disembarking troops.*

△ *The aerial assault operations usually involve a variable number of transport helicopters to move the main body of troops and other reconnaissance and attack helicopters in support.*

Many missions

Helicopters are classified as light, medium or heavy, according to their cargo capacity. The most vital characteristics are high mobility and flexibility. Basically, helicopters can be employed in:

- Tactical missions including the transport of troops to points of maximum concentration to carry out a decisive push, to occupy strategically important points, in anti-guerilla operations, in the interception of enemy troops, to cover the flanks of troop formations and other actions.

- Logistic mission requiring the transport of materiel that is either deposited from the landed helicopter of launched from the air over the combat zone.

Infiltration and air-transport

Infiltration and exfiltration of combat troops depends on very-low flying helicopters which use ground-hugging capabilities to avoid detection, often coupled with night-flying to lessen visual contact. Other types of missions include long-range reconnaissance and the capture of enemy personnel and materiel.

With respect to air-transport missions, helicopters can be used to move ammunition, rations, fuel and other cargoes. The heaviest models are used to move artillery pieces to avoid enemy counter-fire or to deploy contingents to specific points rapidly.

AMERICAN NAVAL
HELICOPTERS

The desire of American naval strategists to achieve domination of the sea led them to begin, in the 1950s, a program of military expansion that was based on the establishment of powerful aircraft-carrier groups. To protect them, it was planned to use frigates and destroyers that would be equipped with helicopters specialized in tasks of detection and destruction of enemy submarines.

Implantation

At the beginning of the 1950s, the Piasechi HUP-2S Retriever, HRS-2 and HSS-1 Seaba entered service. After experimenting with these designs, in December, 1957, the US Navy ordered ten advanced helicopters designated the YHSS-2, from Sikorsky. This evolved to the SH-3A Sea King designed to locate and destroy submarines.

Purchasing

In parallel to the entry into service of the first batch of 254 SH-3A Sea King, the Navy began to receive the Kaman HU-2A Seasprite, light helicopters assigned to naval search and rescue missions. Shortly afterwards, it was decided to optimize the Sea King, with the upgraded SH-3D which had more powerful engines and more modern systems such as the AQS-13A sonar and the APN-182 Doppler-pulse radar, entering service in 1967.

The introduction of the LAMPS (Light Airborne Multi Purpose System) concept at the beginning of the 1970s was the result of the modification of a batch of twenty Seasprite, which were designated the SH-2D. These helicopters were equipped with Canadian Marconi LN-66HP surface search radar in a ventral dome under the cockpit or a MAD Texas Instruments ASQ-81 magnetic anomaly detector in an exterior mount.

Improvements

Until 1982, more than a hundred helicopters were modified to the SH-2F standard, which included a new rotor and modifications in the retractable landing gear. In addition some 116 older helicopters were upgraded to the SH-3H standard.

The same year, manufacturing began of the first production units of the SH-60B Seahawk LAMPS Mk III, whose five prototypes had been undergoing validation since 1979.

The introduction of this advanced helicopter, which began to serve on aircraft carriers from 1991 onwards meant that some SH-3H were retired from service.

For improved protection of naval groups and to equip the modern destroyer, the SH-60F model for close protection of battle groups was designed. The most advanced version is designated the SH-60R. Following the example of the US Navy, many countries have purchased these naval helicopters. The SH-2G Super Seasprite has been bought by Egypt, New Zealand and Australia, which like Spain, Japan, Greece, Thailand and Taiwan has also purchased versions of the SH-60. The SH-3 is active in countries such as Argentina, Belgium, Italy, India or Pakistan.

The SH-3 continues to fulfill many missions effectively, although new designs, all of them variants of the SH-60 are being considered as replacements.

Different performance

The capacities of each model differ according to their equipment and the era when they were designed.

Extraordinary capacity

Without a doubt, the most advanced and expensive of all these helicopters is the Seahawk whose design includes:

- A tried and tested structure.

- Two powerful General Electric T700-GE-410 engines.

- The RAST recovery system which facilitates landings on the deck of escort ships.

- Very advanced avionics.

The different configurations can include:

-Surface-search radar.

- Sonar buoy launchers.

- Acoustic processors.

- Variable-depth, low-frequency sonar.

Along the same lines as the Seahawk, the recently introduced Super Seasprite is much cheaper but has satisfactory mission capacities due to its modern equipment that allows it to perform multiple naval attack missions. Lastly, the different models of the Sea King have, in spite of upgrades, limitations derived from their design and size.

Powerful

The capacity of sea-borne helicopters allows them to identify both submarine and surface targets and destroy them with their own weapons or transmit target information to the mother ship. Their weaponry can include:

- Light 324 mm torpedoes.

- Depth charges, including those with nuclear charges.

- Light anti-ship missiles.

	SH-3 Sea King	SH-2F Seasprite	SH-60B Seahawk
Cost (millions of dollars)	14 millions	12 millions	30 millions
Dimensions:			
Length	22,21 m	16,03 m	19,76 m
Height	5,13 m	4,72 m	5,18 m
Diameter main rotor	18,90 m	13,40 m	16,36 m
Main rotor turning surface	280,48 m²	141,26 m²	210,14 m²
Weight:			
Empty	5.447 kg	3.193 kg	6.191 kg
Maximum	9.752 kg	6.123 kg	9.926 kg
Maximum load weapons	1.300 kg	500 kg	500 kg
Fuel	3.714 l	1.779 l	2.233 l
Power:	3.320 CV	2.700 CV	3.380 CV
Performance:			
Service ceiling	4.410 m	6.860 m	5.790 m
Maximum speed	272 km/h	230 km/h	272 km/h
Range	1.482 km	661 km	600 km

EUROPEAN NAVAL
HELICOPTERS

The European aviation industry has developed several generations of naval helicopters. They have usually been sea-borne helicopters which carry out anti-submarine (ASW) or anti-surface (ASuW) warfare tasks, as well as long-distance reconnaissance, re-supply duties, MEDEVAC (MEDical EVACuation) missions or troop transport.

In the 1950s and 1960s, American helicopters were manufactured under license in Europe, and this was the launching pad for an industry that has developed the capacity to bring to the market some of the most advanced current designs.

An evolving process

In 1959, the British firm Westland obtained a license to manufacture the American Sikorsky S-61/SH-3 Sea King for supply to the Royal Navy. Over the years, variants such as the air-detection model with Searchwater radar and the Commando troop-transport have been produced.

After constructing the SH-3 and various Bell helicopters under license, the Italian firm

Agusta S.p.A. manufactured the 212 model in a version destined for anti-submarine warfare and designated the AB-212. More than a hundred have been sold to the navies of Italy, Greece, Iraq, Turkey, Venezuela and Spain.

Self-sufficiency

The development of European designs has benefited from the process of manufacturing, optimizing and adapting models in service. The first to be presented was the Lynx light helicopter, which was a collaboration between France (30%) and the United Kingdom (70%). Production began in 1976 and the current model is known as the 300 or Super Lynx. To replace the first Lynx and some Sea King helicopters, Westland and Agusta

signed a development protocol in 1979 for a new model. The result was the EH-101 Merlin which first flew in October, 1987, with the first production series being purchased by the United Kingdom, Italy and Canada towards the end of the 20th century. The European industry has also produced models such as the powerful French Super Frelon or the lighter Eurocopter AS 365N3 Dauphin 2, which have been purchased by various countries.

Details

Each of the helicopters mentioned has been produced in a different era and with different operational objectives, giving rise to widely different characteristics.

▶ The Lynx is a small helicopter of which many have been sold and which is still serving in countries such as the United Kingdom, the Netherlands and Portugal.

◀ The French Dauphin are light-medium helicopters which can fulfill rescue missions and other tasks.

AB-212 ASW

Made by Augusta in Italy, this derivation of the AB-205 for naval use incorporates changes in the structure that permit its adaptation to different operational requirements. It includes:

- A Pratt & Whitney Canada PT6T-6 Turbo Twin Pac engine.
- Surface-search radar located in the cylindrical container over the cockpit.
- Variable-depth, low-frequency AQS-18 sonar.

- A digital data presentation array.
- A reinforced rust-resistant structure.
- Skids with floats for emergency sea landings.
- Reinforced deck moorings.

Lynx

This small helicopter British-French helicopter was designed using a fuselage made of light alloy with doors, access panels and other elements of glass-fiber. The characteristics include:

- A non-retractable tricycle tailwheel type landing gear.
- A cockpit with all-weather equipment.
- Two Rolls-Royce Gem 2 engines.
- A cargo capacity of twelve troops.

The British helicopters include:
- Sistema GPS.
- A GPS system.
- A GEC-Marconi surface-search radar with the capacity to locate small targets in low visibility and rough seas.

▲ *The US Coast Guard uses European helicopters including the Dauphin, with positive results.*

Technical Characteristics

	AB-212 ASW	Lynx	EH-101 Merlin
Cost (millions of dollars):	12 millions	22 millions	35 millions
Dimensions:			
Length fuselage	17,40 m	15,17 m	22,81 m
Height	4,53 m	3,48 m	6,62 m
Diameter main rotor	14,63 m	12,80 m	18,59 m
Main rotor turning surface	173,90 m²	128,71 m²	271,51 m²
Weight:			
Empty	3.240 kg	2.740 kg	7.121 kg
Maximum	5.070 kg	4.876 kg	14.600 kg
Maximum load weapons	800 kg	700 kg	960 kg
Fuel	814 l	957 l	3.222 l
Power:	1.875 CV	2.240 CV	6.936 CV
Performance:			
Service ceiling	4.023 m	3.230 m	5.000 m
Maximum speed	196 km/h	232 km/h	278 km/h
Range	667 km	500 km	900 km

- Nose-mounted thermal imaging.
- Radar detection systems.

The French helicopters are armed with:
- Light Mùrene torpedoes.
- Depth charges.
- AS-15TT anti-ship missiles.

Merlin

The Merlin is a third-generation naval helicopter.
- The Merlin is a very large helicopter with a fuselage of aluminum, lithium, composite materials and sandwich panels.
- It can perform naval take-offs in winds of up to 90 km/h and in force 6 seas.
- It incorporates a system of automatic coupling when landing.
- The main rotor can be inclined to a negative angle to facilitate landing in extreme conditions.
- The two crewmembers have Martin-Baker armored seats and a six-panel multifunction data array.
- The submarine and surface location sensors are among the most advanced in the world.

The need to give support to ground forces has meant, the need for helicopters, from the first models onwards, to be equipped with various weapons systems. Today, after the combat validation of various concepts, the implantation of specialized variants of air-to-surface and air-to-air weapons has become generalized, although all models can be equipped with offensive weapons.

Machine guns and cannons

The most-simple weaponry, cheap and easy to use, is a lateral rotating mount that facilitates the sweeping movement of the machine gun. More complex and with greater capacity are mounts such as the American M134 which comprises six rotating guns that fire 7.62x51 mm ammunition at a rate of up to 6,000 shots per minute. The types used include:
  - The Rheinmetall Rh-202 20 mm gun used by the Spanish BO-105.
  - The GIAT M621 used in French Puma transport helicopters.
Even more powerful are the 20 or 30 mm guns used both from fuselage mounts and from integrated turrets. These include:
  - The three-barrel M197 used on the Cobra.
  - The multi-purpose 30 mm M230 Chain Gun of the Apache.
  - The Soviet 2A42 30 mm gun installed in the Mi-28 Havoc.

Rocket-launchers and other systems

There are various economical, simple-to-use, models of rocket-launchers on the market. Basically, these consist of a container which houses a variable number of rockets that are launched against specific surface targets with the help of some kind of aiming system.

◄ The EC635 is one of the new generation of light helicopters and can be equipped with considerable offensive weapon capabilities.

▼ Missiles such as the AS-15TT have a range of around 10 km Launched from helicopters such as this Dauphin, they are usually employed against light naval targets.

▲ The Norwegian Penguin are medium-range anti-ship missiles which are used by various countries to equip American SH-60 helicopters.

◄ Recent years have seen the proliferation of pods containing 20 mm guns and their ammunition, an economical and easily-installed system for medium-lift transport helicopters.

The models range from 37 mm to 81 mm, although the most widely-used are the 68 and 70mm (2,75") models. The rockets follow a straight trajectory and have a range of around 2 km. Also available are containers for anti-tank mines or automatic 40 mm grenade-launchers, which are fired at a distance or managed by a gunner and can fire at a rate of up to 200 shots per minute, being effective against unarmored or lightly-armored vehicles.

Missiles
More-difficult targets require the use of guided missiles with a greater destructive capacity and accuracy, even against moving targets.
Those used in attack helicopters include anti-tank missiles that are guided to the target by their own warhead or by a system controlled from the helicopter. The missiles are classified as long-range up to 4 km and very long-range if they cover a greater distance.
The models currently available include:
 - The French-German HOT.
 - The American TOW and Hellfire.
 - The Russian Spiral.
 - The South-African Swift.
 - The Maverik, which has an extremely long range.
In air-to-air combat other missiles can be used, such as:
 - The French Mistra.
 - The American Stinger.
 - The South-African V3 Kukri.
 - The British Startreak.

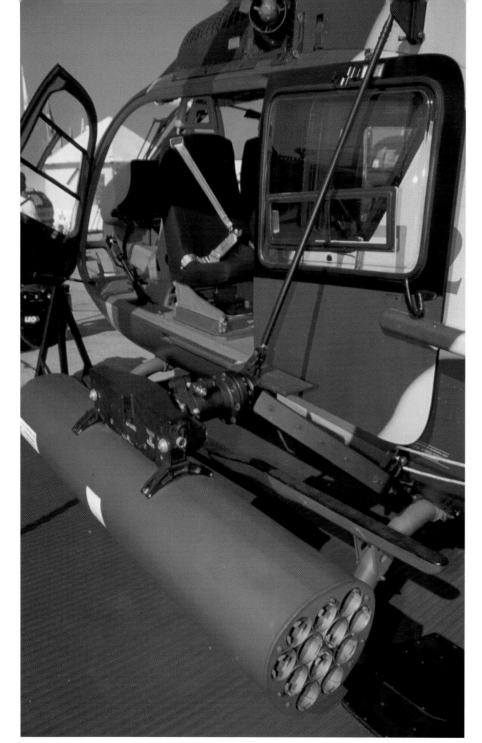

- The Chinese QW-1.
- The Russian SA-7 Grail, SA-14 Gremlin, SA-16 Gimlet and SA-18 Grouse.

These missiles are capable of downing other helicopters or older aircraft.

Naval weapons

Submarines can be attacked with machine guns, cannons and rockets when they surface. Underwater attacks require specialized light torpedoes, generally 324 mm, such as:

- The American Mk-46 and Mk-50.

- The Swedish Type 43.
- The Italian A-244/S, which has a range of 6.5 km.
- The British Sting Ray.

For attacks on surface vessels, helicopters are equipped with anti-ship missiles. Missiles guided from the helicopter, with a range of less than 20 km include:

- The Aerospatiale AS-15TT.
- The British Sea Skua.
- The Norwegian Penguin.
- The Italian Marte 2.

Self-guided missiles with a range of over 50 km include:

- The AM.39 Exocet, used from the French Super Frelon.
- The British Sea Eagle, used from the Indian navy Sea Kings.

Helicopters can also be used as vectors for mine-laying operations, using weapons such as:

- The British light Mk11.
- The American Mk36 or B57 with a nuclear warhead.
- The Swedish SAM 204.

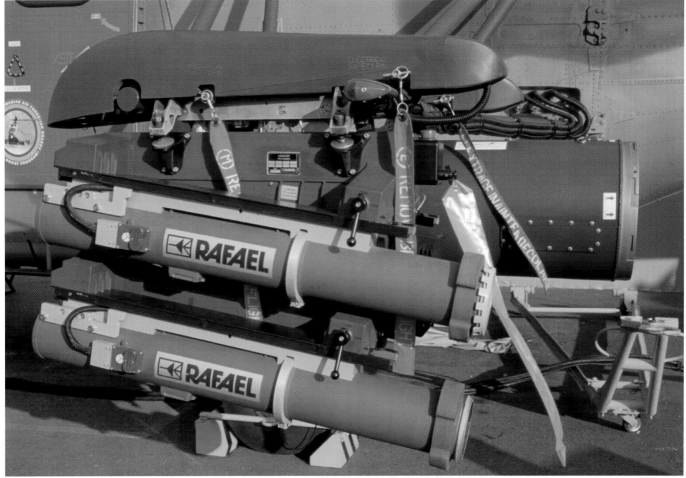

Photo credits:

Boeing:
12, 13

Japan Ministry of Defense:
61

Octavio Díez:
07, 10, 11, 16, 17, 34, 35, 41, 42, 43, 46, 47, 49, 62, 63, 68, 73, 89, 94, 95

Remaining photographies:
Aerospatiale Matra, Agusta-Westland, Bell/Agusta, Bell Helicopter, Boeing, Octavio Díez,
DoD, Eurocopter, MBDA, Australian Ministry of Defense, UK Ministry of Defense, Sikorsky,
US Air Force, US Marines, US Navy.